CITROËN
2CV
THE FAMILY ALBUM

This book is dedicated to Eve Sparrow, in memory of my father James Sparrow,
who died just before it was completed

Other books available from Veloce -

Alfa Romeo Tipo 6C 1500, 1750 & 1900
by Angela Cherrett
Alfa Romeo Modello 8C 2300
by Angela Cherrett
Alfa Romeo Giulia Coupé GT & GTA
by John Tipler
BIGGLES! The Life Story of Captain W. E. Johns
by Peter Berresford Ellis & Jennifer Schofield
British Car Factories from 1896 - A Complete Survey
by Paul Collins & Michael Stratton
Bugatti 57 - The Last French Bugatti
by Barrie Price
Fiat & Abarth 124 Spider & Coupé
by John Tipler
Standard & Standard-Triumph - The Illustrated History
by Brian Long
The Prince & I - My Life With The Motor Racing Prince Of Siam
(Biography of racing driver 'B. Bira') by Princess Ceril Birabongse
The Car Security Manual
by David Pollard
Total Tuning for the Classic MG Midget/A-H Sprite
by Daniel Stapleton

First published in 1993 by Veloce Publishing Plc, Godmanstone, Dorset DT2 7AE, England.
Fax: 0300 341065

ISBN 1 874105 13 8

Readers with ideas for automotive books, or books on other transport or related hobby subjects, are invited to write to the Editorial Director of Veloce Publishing at the above address.

British Library Cataloguing In Publication Data -
A catalogue record for this book is available from the British Library.

Typesetting (in Avant Garde, Times & Technical), design and page make-up all by Veloce on Apple Mac.

Printed in Singapore by PH Productions Pte Ltd.

CITROËN 2CV

THE FAMILY ALBUM

ANDREA & DAVID SPARROW

VELOCE PUBLISHING PLC

PUBLISHERS OF FINE AUTOMOTIVE BOOKS

THANKS

Thanks are due to the following for their help -

France: Mme Agrel Hoeg, Florence Lebottel & Marcel Allard of Citroen Paris, Daniel Girod-Roux.

Great Britain: Nick Thompson of Sussex 2CV, Ray Williams of Burnham, Chantelle and Heidi Jones, Jenny Irving, Thomas Eckered, Steve Hill, David Adams, John Miller, Malcolm Henry, Mike & Pat Lancaster, Colin Cusworth, Larry Griffiths, Julia Bragg, Richard Nelson, Mark & Pamela Haynes, Lesley Cooke, Malcolm Blanksby, Jane Dixon, Janice McHardy, David & Marion Lanham, Sarah and Roger Keable, Jennifer Leslie, Jane Tweed, Jeremy Moss, Peter Harper, Trevor Richardson, Jon Colley, Roy Eastwood, Julia Hodgkin, Simon Thomas, Leigh Gooding, David Conway, Carole Stevens, Andrew Minney, Joanna Kelly, P&O Ferries.

Netherlands: Frans van de Water, Tim van Daal, Gert Jan Pelt, Joost Jager, Willem Aal, Martin Punter, Esther Pangemanen, Lies Linnekamp, Marcel Koops, Sandra, Paul-Frank Moerman, Bouwen & Susan Scheygrond, Johan & Joke van der Wal, Paul van den Berg, Gerard Snijders, Rene Vas, Ellen & Henk Bovenkerk, Marcel van Schaik, P J Goverde, Paul Verwey, Hans & Loes Monsee, Hettie Haan, Henk van Wezel, F H Friederich, Peter van Velzen, Annelies Kamerbeek, C P de Haan, M W Goeree, Ton de Graaf, the Koolmees family, Andre van Wageningen, Trudy Hermans. Special thanks are due to Jan de Lange.

Switzerland: Alfred Gut.

CONTENT

THE FRENCH CONNECTION

The early days of the 2CV were coloured blue and yellow. The distinctive Citroën livery was to be seen above the door of many a workshop in towns and villages throughout France.

But the original colour of the 2CV was grey. Dark grey at the beginning, with grey wheels and only later a little light relief; lighter grey with a pale yellow tinge to the wheels. It was a car for the working man or woman, for the farmer: a car that had to be able to carry sacks of potatoes. But times change and, in later years, the 2CV has developed a double personality.

The agricultural French 2CV still exists. It's not hard to find. A drive through the gallic countryside will soon yield that familiar sight; the rounded fabric top peeping above the hedge, a glimpse of familiar round headlight between farm buildings. The Camionette can still be found in the village square delivering fresh bread. The weathered example in matt blue with obligatory dents and one green wing is still parked outside the bar every evening.

Yet in both Holland and England, the 2CV found its niche as a town car rather than a country one. True, Dutch 2CVs found favour as one of the few vehicles light enough to travel safely over still-marshy reclaimed land, but their natural habitat in these countries seems to be in town. Perhaps it is for this reason that the more modern special editions, while popular in France too, have been particularly well received elsewhere?

The first special edition 2CV was called SPOT - an acronym for SPecial Orange Ténéré. It was produced in 1976, at the start of the craze for special editions. It was really a car of white and orange sections with stuck-on coachstripes: the seats and hood in orange and white stripes continued the theme.

By the early 1980s, nostalgia reigned supreme. The 2CV Charleston was originally a limited edition, but proved so popular with its Delage red and black livery that it soon became a part of the standard range on offer. The following year, a yellow and black version appeared, followed by a tasteful grey and black. Although popular, these two later versions have never sold as well as the original.

Ten years later tastes were less fussy, more stylish. Enter the

An English 2CV shows its favourite colours.

Dolly, a car in two contrasting colours, in seven different versions. This 2CV was particularly popular in Britain, indeed it still is, with a special club being run just for Dolly owners. The cars were not generally available in Holland unless by special import. Plain colours remained more popular in France, although the France 3, a white car with blue stripe to its panels and hood, found favour. It was named after a yacht which took part in the Americas' Cup races - and this being of no interest outside its country of origin, it carried the name Beachcomber in England, and Transat in Holland.

SPOT - Special Orange Tenere - the start of 2CV special editions. Produced in 1976 it featured orange and white adhesive bodystripes. Seats and hood were in orange; an orange and white striped sunblind could be pulled forward to provide shade for driver and front seat passenger when the hood was rolled back. Although few Spots survive in good condition, interest in them has revived and a Spot club has been set up to promote them.

The Beachcomber (or France 3/Transat) always attracted eccentric owners.

'X' marks the Spot.

Red, white and blue - the colours of France; the 2CV has always epitomised French character.

The three Charleston colour schemes: Delage red and black - the first colour scheme, the most conservative combination and the most popular. Sales of this very nostalgic car far surpassed Citroen's expectations. Unconventional, fun, and standing out from the crowd, the yellow and black Charleston is nevertheless a very smart car indeed. The grey and black Charleston version is quieter, more understated and classy.

All the seven versions of Dolly that were ever produced. The rarest is grey and white.

Below: Do owners think of their 2CVs as male or female? Dolly, however, is most definitely a

lady, billed in her early publicity material as a 'Show-business queen'.

2CV a car for the town. Opposite page, under the old Cathedral tower in Utrecht; above, a choice of places to eat in a Loire valley town; left, the colleges of Oxford ...

... or early Sunday morning in Brighton.

A car for the country. Below, a 2CV owner for the 21st century perhaps; opposite & above, both old and new - beside the sea ...

... alongside the waterways of Holland ...

... or an original 1957 French car in an English landscape - Arundel Castle in Sussex.

ANCESTORS

The father of the 2CV was Pierre Boulanger. Following the death of André Citroën in 1935, Boulanger and Pierre Michelin, who had met during the First World War, took over the running of the firm, which needed a sound injection of expertise and enthusiasm to get it going again after a turbulent period of unprofitability and liquidation. Boulanger inherited a team who had previously worked on the Traction Avant, including the designer André Lefebvre and stylist Bertoni. Having assured himself that there was a market for such a car, Boulanger set the ball rolling. His ideas for a small car were taken on board by the team; the project was called TPV (for Toute Petite Voiture). They were to come up with a car that weighed less than 300 kilos, in order that running costs could be kept down. By 1936 they had made a wooden model, and within twelve months were assessing the success of the first prototype. This was powered by a 500cc BMW motorcycle engine. Its drive train came courtesy of its big brother the Traction Avant, with much of the bodywork being made of aluminium for

maximum lightness.

During that year they made 20 prototypes, which they tested rigorously - not a job for the faint hearted, as the aluminium made the whole affair too light and it went too fast for its own (and its driver's) good! During the months that followed, there were other problems and Pierre Michelin was killed in a road accident. Aluminium proved a less than satifactory medium to work in. Solutions to some of the handling problems were resulting in a steady gain in weight. The team had not produced a particularly user-friendly machine in the DIY department: a ramp or pit was necessary in order to put oil in the engine!

Boulanger's aim was to unveil the car at the Paris Motor Show in late 1939. The plan was to make 250 cars ready for the event and on 2nd September the first car was finished. The following day, however, war was declared and everything, the TPV project included, was thrown into a state of turmoil. Very little could be done to the car under occupation; Boulanger's moral standpoint was that there should be no co-operation with the Nazis, and he ordered that the cars already built, or partially so, should be destroyed to prevent any ideas getting into enemy hands. Despite the difficulties, he managed to review the TPV project for cost and feasability and, towards the end of the war, a new air cooled engine was designed to replace the problematic water-cooled one that had powered the pre-war prototypes.

It was finally decided to show the car at the Paris show of 1948, and cars were produced accordingly. They came in one colour - a metallic grey. Boulanger introduced his 2CV, as it was to be called, to the astonishment of press and public alike. There had never been anything quite like it before. Nor perhaps has there been since. The one part of the car that remained a closed secret was the engine. Boulanger ensured that the bonnets were sealed at the show - to prevent incursions from the Renault stand next door, one assumes - since he knew that his cars would not be readily available for some time, and had no intention of letting a competitor steal a march on him.

Production got underway in

Ordered to be destroyed when war broke out, yet surviving for thirty years as components packed in crates, this 1939 prototype has been reconstructed and lovingly restored. On later prototypes the single headlamp was provided with a nearside partner because test drivers found their cars being mistaken for oncoming motorbikes in the dark.

earnest in 1949. By the time the 2CV was shown at that year's show the bonnet not only opened but, along with the front wings, was completely removed on some cars. The cost of the car was 228,000 francs, 25% more than had originally been intended. But it was hugely popular with its intended market of working people. The war was over, but austerity was still the keyword. The little car represented just the kind of economical operation that was needed as the country began slowly to put itself back on its feet. Members of the motoring press could afford to sneer at it, but many did appreciate it for exactly what it was; a first class way of bringing ac-

ceptably-priced motorised transport to those who needed it most.

There is one survivor of the pre-war TPV era living a quiet life of seclusion in Paris. In 1970, Citroën's chief of publicity, Jacques Wolgensinger, rediscovered parts of one of the original 250 prototypes stored in crates. He had it reconstructed, and it is now housed at Citroën headquarters in Neuilly. Unmistakably 2CV, its appearance is nevertheless unique. At the front - deeply ridged bonnet and engine cover with chevrons incorporated, single round headlamp, starting handle permanently attached. From the sides - semi-circular rear door, both doors hinged at the central pillar, exposed rear wheel, mica windows. Inside - hammock-style seats hung on steel wires, with brown canvas seats and tan seat cushions which match the canvas hood. The engine is the original water-cooled version which is maintained in perfect running order. The car is charming; odd in that it looks more like a caricature of an older 2CV than anything - slightly severe in demeanor due to its military colouring, but dignified none the less, like an old soldier.

The original rear door was a complete semi-circle; the shape reappeared in the paintwork of the Charleston forty years later.

No other 2CV engine looks quite like this - the radiator comes courtesy of the Traction Avant.

AT WORK

When the idea of the 2CV was first conceived by Pierre Boulanger the intention was clear: it should be a car that would meet the needs of, and appeal to, the ordinary working person - giving him or her a mobility that would previously have been the prerogative of the more wealthy. He was convinced that there was a niche for a small car, inexpensive to buy and to run. He summed up his initial thoughts on the car as 'a settee under an umbrella'. To his design team he issued very tight instructions. The car was to carry two farmers dressed for work and fifty kilos of potatoes or a small barrel of wine. The car must carry them in reasonable comfort over the very worst of roads at no more than 60 Km/hour. It would use no more than three litres of petrol to cover 100Km. Repair and maintenance costs had to be kept to a minimum - it would be no use if a replacement tyre were to part an owner from ten per cent of his monthly earnings.

By way of market research, more than ten thousand working folk were interviewed. They were asked what sort of transport would meet their requirements, how much could they

afford to spend - what features would be important to them and which would matter not at all.

When the first 2CVs became available in 1949, numbers were limited, and a waiting list of twelve months or so soon formed. True to his original concept of a car for working people, Boulanger insisted that those with the greatest need of them - doctors, midwives etc - should have priority. Would-be buyers could expect a visit from a gentleman from Citroën asking them questions to assess their positioning on the list.

The freedom which the car created was something quite new. A country doctor might be able to afford a large automobile - but its usefulness would be restricted by lack of good roads - in some places by lack of any roads at all! The farmer would previously have had to haul his wares to market in a large and cumbersome car which his wife might prefer not to drive. He then had to wait in town, using up valuable daylight hours (and spending money in the local hostelry to pass the time!), while his wife sold their produce. The advent of the 2CV changed all this. The farmer's wife could drive herself to market and back with no problems. There would be plenty of room for farm produce; the canvas top could be rolled back if necessary. Nothing would get damaged because one of the first criteria set for the car was that it should be able to cross a ploughed field with a basket of eggs on the rear seat and that none should be broken in transit.

The car found immediate popularity with farmers, vets, doctors, shopkeepers and tradespeople of every kind.

More than thirty years later in 1961, the van version of the 2CV, the Camionette, was publicised with the aid of a comprehensive brochure depicting various occupations and their associated cargo. A milliner with hat boxes galore in all sizes - a florist, decorator, photographer, plumber, farmer, baker and greengrocer - each with the accoutrements of their trade - and all owing their success to the car. A commercial variant version of the 2CV was available as early as 1951 in France, where it was known as the Fourgonette.

An early advertisement pointed out that the van possessed all the amenities of a car with all the advantages of a delivery truck. Thanks to the soft suspension, no special packaging of breakable goods was required.

The Vans, with their distinctive corrugated sides, were manufactured by Panhard. They have remained a popular feature of the rural landscape of France, delivering bread or vegetables or at work in farmyards and fields. The French post office, PTT, ran fleets of bright yellow vans for many years. A 'Week-end' version of the 2CV van was produced; it had a second window in the side and an extra row of seats which were removable. Thus it lived a

"It's the car that is most suited to the needs of daily life. It interests people in all walks of life and meets all their demands." (1971 Citroen brochure describing 2CV4)

The village baker was an early customer for the 2CV, the van version being particularly popular.

The smell of freshly baked bread, crumbling croissants, mouth-watering patisserie, all delivered by 2CV.

double life - workhorse during the week and family runabout at weekends. Pick-up versions have also appeared from time to time - mainly they were simple cut-downs of the van and found considerable favour with the French army, by virtue of being helicopter-transportable; thirty right hand drive examples were supplied to the British Admiralty in the late 1950s.

Strange, weird and wonderful working cars to suit particular purposes should also be mentioned: an Estate version of spectacular ugliness hailed from Iran and Spain, the Citronetta, half 2CV-half box, emerged from Chile. Closer to home, ENAC produced what was effectively a 2CV hatchback, with hinges above the rear window and folding rear seats, called the Mixte.

In 1978 the 2CV van version was discontinued in favour of the Acadiene, built on an elongated chassis, with Dyane front panels. This too has become extremely popular in France, and has achieved success in other countries never attained by the earlier versions.

More than forty years after its introduction the little Citroën van can still be found making its mark on the world of commerce - selling everything from saucepans to sandwiches, geraniums to gateaux, curtains to crustacia.

The van version of the 2CV is often referred to as Camionette, Fourgonette or Kombi. It proved very popular with small businesses of all kinds, both in France and elsewhere in Europe. The Dyane version, Acadiene, is a very popular working car too.

Quite a family get-together; 2CV, Camionette, Mehari, Ami - and, presumably, half of deux chevaux?

In the warm climate of southern France, an elderly 2CV can survive without suffering unduly from rust, although dented wings and bent grilles are simply an occupational hazard of being a working 2CV.

Panhard produced their own cars at Avenue d'Ivry, at the same time as they were building Citroen's commercials. The Dyna 54 (or type Z1) was the hit of the 1953 Paris Salon, and was powered by Panhard's own 850cc twin-cylinder air-cooled engine driving the front wheels.

Due to their corrugated appearance, the early vans were often scorned by detractors as 'tin sheds on wheels' - but to their many owners they were a cheap and convenient way of carrying substantial loads with ease.

AT PLAY

Although the 2CV was conceived and designed with the working person in mind, it was obviously going to have repercussions in his or her social life too. Early advertisements show families packed into their 2CV for a Sunday outing. Children wave through the rolled-back roof. The seats are removed to provide comfortable seating for a family picnic next to the river. This new frugal little car brought with it a greater freedom of movement. A family motoring trip to the Mont-St-Michel, or to Paris, perhaps, could be considered a real possibility.

It was inevitable that the 2CV was going to find itself at the centre of many weird and wonderful escapades. One of the first was a circuit of the Mediterranean undertaken by one Michel Bernier. In 1953, Jacques Cornet and Henri Lochon, who both worked for Citroën, set off on a marathon run from northern Canada to Terra del Fuego. In the year that their journey took they covered 52,000 kilometres, beating the world altitude record for a motor car while passing through Bolivia. In 1959, Jacques Seguela and Lean-Claude Baudot covered 100,000 kilome-

tres in the course of a round the world trip in a 2CV. Their journey started at the Paris Motor Show, ten years after the first 2CVs became available there.

In the late 'sixties and early 'seventies, Citroën organised a series of adventure trips, called 'raids'. 1969 found 25 Meharis making the 15,000Km trip from Liége to Dakar and back. For the following year's trip, an invitation was issued to 2CV owners wishing to take part. There was an enormous response. 1300 people in 500 cars traversed 18 countries; part of their raid retracing the route of an earlier Citroën expedition - called the Croisiere Jaune - which took place in 1931/32. This marathon journey involved two groups of Citroën cars travelling one group from either end of the Asian continent from Beirut and Peking. In 1971 a raid was organised from Paris to Persepolis in Iran by way of Italy, Yugoslavia, Greece and Turkey; the response to these events was now so great that not everyone wishing to take part could do so. A year later, and the stiffest of all these challenges was announced: the crossing of the remote and formidable Ténéré desert.

In 2CV Cross bits fall off, and bits are put back on again: the availability of spare parts and panels makes the sport readily accessible to all; although not expensive, it is taken seriously by drivers and clubs alike.

Accompanied by back-up lorries with mechanics, doctors and helpers, the cars set out in groups. After a month of hard work and 8000Km of arduous driving, all the participants arrived safely in Tunis.

In 1972, a new kind of leisure activity was invented by Citroën themselves. Based around the plentious supply of relatively cheap 2CVs, and the ease of taking them apart and bolting them back together again, the sport was originally called 'Pop-Cross.' The first meeting was held at Argenton-sur-Creuse in a disused quarry especially prepared for the purpose. This very

accessible form of motorsport caught on very quickly, and its popularity spread rapidly both in France and throughout Europe, especially in Holland. The first such event in Britain was held in 1975. Clubs were formed, initially to run the meetings on Citroën's behalf, although they later completely took over the organisation of what is now known as 2CV Cross. Regulations restrict the sport to 2CVs of original specification; modifications are strictly controlled, with no increasing of the engine's power allowed. The cars must be fitted with roll cages and harnesses to protect the driver.

The glass is removed, and a metal windscreen grille fitted. The back doors are removed - the front ones and boot being welded shut. The chassis is reinforced, and the suspension may be modified slightly. Despite all appearances to the contrary, 2CV Cross is actually a very safe sport; maximum speeds are no more than 70Km/hour. Only five litres of petrol are ever carried at one time, and a special valve fitted to the filler pipe keeps the fuel inside even if the car is upside down!

If such adventures seem a little on the severe side, there are other forms of leisure to which the 2CV is ably suited: a quiet drive in the country, a journey to the seaside; trips to smart hotels or a quiet cafés. The Acadiene commercial version of the 2CV is popular as a motorhome conversion too. With judicious use of space and a tidy approach to life, the little van makes an excellent week-end and holiday companion.

2CV Cross has become popular not only with participants and spectators, but with sponsors too.

Safety rules insist on a roll cage, one seat, and the removal of all glass.

Although the sport looks alarming - and the 2CV's tendency to lean makes it appear more so - there are very few serious accidents or injuries.

The dog and duck; one dog and his ducks.

One woman
and her duck
and dog.

The 2CV will wait for you outside the most upmarket hotel ... or is equally at home outside the local cafe.

On top of the world with a 2CV.

The seats of a 2CV can be removed for picnics.

A bird of a
different
feather.

CLOSE RELATIONS

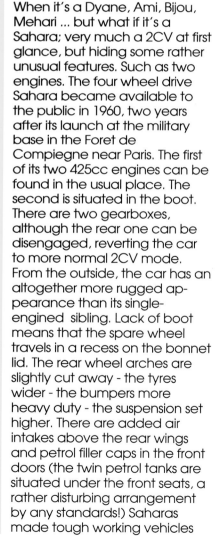

When is as 2CV not a 2CV? When it's a Dyane, Ami, Bijou, Mehari ... but what if it's a Sahara; very much a 2CV at first glance, but hiding some rather unusual features. Such as two engines. The four wheel drive Sahara became available to the public in 1960, two years after its launch at the military base in the Foret de Compiegne near Paris. The first of its two 425cc engines can be found in the usual place. The second is situated in the boot. There are two gearboxes, although the rear one can be disengaged, reverting the car to more normal 2CV mode. From the outside, the car has an altogether more rugged ap-pearance than its single-engined sibling. Lack of boot means that the spare wheel travels in a recess on the bonnet lid. The rear wheel arches are slightly cut away - the tyres wider - the bumpers more heavy duty - the suspension set higher. There are added air intakes above the rear wings and petrol filler caps in the front doors (the twin petrol tanks are situated under the front seats, a rather disturbing arrangement by any standards!) Saharas made tough working vehicles

and found favour in Switzerland as snow-clearers and as vital transport for doctors and the like, who might otherwise be snowbound. Some found their way to the deserts of North Africa, and the Spanish Police were an unlikely customer for 80 of them. Despite this popularity, only 700 or so Saharas were ever built.

1961. Time for something new. Both Renault and Peugeot were bringing out new models. The basic ideas behind the 2CV still held good, but Citroën wanted to introduce something a little more modern in the saleability stakes. Enter the Ami 6 - economical to run, it was based on the 2CV chassis but with a 602cc engine. It was comfortable to sit in and to drive, and instantly found favour with the French car-buyer. Indeed, it was France's best-selling car at one point. Its attributes were simplicity and style, it was thought smart but practical - it was certainly idiosyncratic to look at.

1964 brought an Estate version, which was capable of taking quite substantial loads with ease. The Ami 8 replaced the 6 in 1969 - although it looked very different, its insides, both cabin and engine-wise, were very similar. The last Ami version to be introduced was the Ami Super, which was driven by the 1000cc engine from the GS range. Ami models were available as 'Tourisme' - the standard version - or 'Confort' - which was better appointed and therefore more expensive. A commercial variant of the Estate car became known as the Enterprise. Ami 8s continued in production until 1979.

From 1949 until 1961, when it was joined by the Ami, the 2CV had reigned alone as the Citroën small car. In 1968 another variation joined the family, the Dyane. This had originally been intended to replace the 2CV, upon whose chassis it was built, although many of its mechanical parts came courtesy of the Ami. Its looks suggested it to be a hybrid of both cars. The first Dyane had the 425cc 2CV engine, which was replaced in 1968 with the 435cc; this was the Dyane 4. The Dyane 6 was fitted with the 602cc from the Ami. When the 4 was discontinued in 1974, a week-end version of the six was added, with the added refinements of folding rear seats and two front ones.

The last Dyanes were produced in 1982; the model never managed the job of replacing the 2CV. With its square, set-in headlamps and more conventional lines than its elder sister, the Dyane was loved by some 2CV fans, loathed by others. But, like the Ami, it has friends all its own, and some special editions were produced, the most often seen being the Côte d'Azur.

From a car named after a goddess to one named after a camel - the Mehari. Designed to be a versatile all-purpose load carrying vehicle, the Mehari began life in 1968 called Dyane Mehari because it was constructed around the standard Dyane chassis with 602cc engine. The body sections, distinctively ridged, were made from reformable self-coloured

The original intention was for the Dyane to replace the 2CV. In the event it failed to do so, but collected a following all its own along the way. This is the only Dyane special edition to make any real impact in Northern Europe: the Côte d'Azur.

plastic. Easy to clean and impervious to small knocks and bumps, the Mehari could cope with all conditions. Early Meharis had two seats, later versions had four. The most popular version, with four wheel drive, was introduced in 1979. The spare wheel sitting atop the recessed bonnet freed more space in the rear, which was capable of taking large loads with ease. Only the windshield of Mehari is made of glass. The coverings for side, back and top are of plasticised fabric, and may be removed completely, as can the doors.

The Mehari formed the basis of several models that were built in other countries, notably the Baby-Brousse and Dalat in Saigon and FAF from Senegal. The Mehari found favour mainly as a working vehicle, especially in the countryside, but it was not without its following as a fun car. Citroën's publicity photographs show its use as a golf cart and beach buggy; for the latter market the only special edition Mehari was brought out - called Azur, it came in white with blue and white striped seats and with a more substantial top.

Although it had its own advantages, many 2CV fans regarded the Dyane as an upstart - something different maybe, but why something different for the sake of it?

59

And so to the strangest, most unlikely 2CV derivative of all - the Bijou. A gem? Perhaps only in the sense of being a rarity - only 200 or so were ever made. When production of the right hand drive 2CV stopped in 1959, Citroën planned to introduce a new little car designed especially for the British market, One of the major criticisms of the 2CV in Britain had been the unconventional look, particularly with regard to the lack of a 'real' boot. So the Bijou was born; a second car, a shopping car by design, with little room in the back, two doors, a boot, a reasonable degree of comfort and economy. It was made of glass fibre, and thus both light and rust-free. Unfortunately, the competition in the small car sector of the British market was both more conventional and cheaper - the Bijou was never going to catch on - it really was a dead duck!

Just like the Dyane, the Ami had, and still has, its particular enthusiasts. This beautifully maintained example comes from Holland.

The car that was supposed to stop the British in their tracks - the Bijou. Its driving position is such that it cannot easily be driven by anyone of above average height. The British market was perceived as needing a shopping car - hence the 'proper' boot.

The Panhard company was bought out by Citroen; there is no doubting the styling influence of the Panhard 24, which was first produced in 1963.

The Ami 6 estate had plenty of load carrying space and the car provided a very good comfortable ride, whether loaded or not.

The four wheel drive version of the Mehari has four seats, although it is often used with the rear two removed. Extra load space is provided by siting the spare on the bonnet. The original Mehari did not have four wheel drive.

Its spare wheel atop the especially recessed bonnet, the two-engined Sahara is ready for anything. As the car's life tended to be hard by its very nature, not many Saharas survive. Note the fuel filler in the door through which the tanks beneath the front seats are filled.

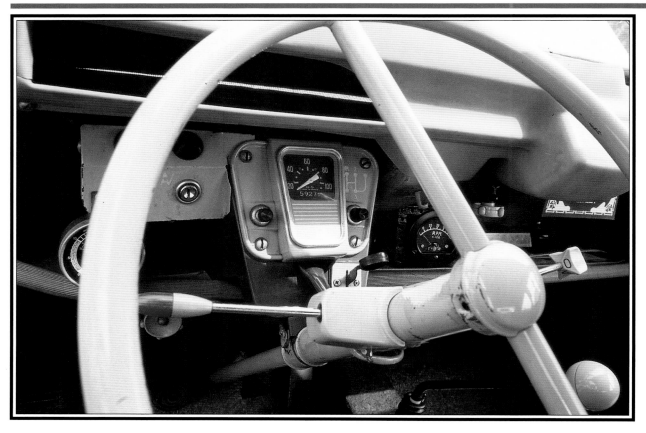

Sahara's dashpanel has two ignition switches (one obscured here by the steering wheel rim)
and between the seats are two choke knobs - one for each engine.

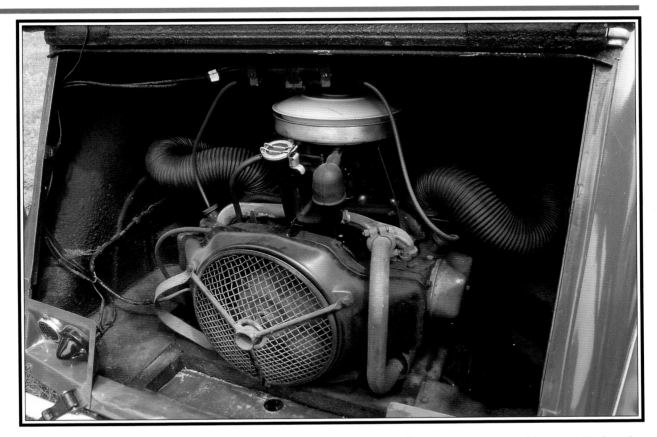

The Sahara's second engine lives in the back of the car where the boot would normally be. A large air intake keeps things cool.

ONE BIG FAMILY

While the basic shape of the 2CV changed not at all during its production life, there was much evolution of detail.

The chevrons which graced the original grille were enclosed in an oval; this combination having been the Citroën symbol for many years. The oval disappeared in 1955 - the chevrons becoming slightly larger and more spidery, looking rather lost on the grille, with the appearance of two corners of a metal picture frame. 1960, and the grille has been redesigned; the chevrons form part of the grillework itself. Six years later they are on the move again; up onto the bonnet this time, above a new style grille with four continuous horizonal bars. 1974, and they move back - incorporated again, but this time neatly, in a grille of grey plastic.

There have been only two types of bonnet. Before 1961 it had 23 parallel ridges from windscreen to just above the grille, rounded slightly to a point in the centre. After 1961, there are only five corrugations; they converge from the screen towards the base of the grille. With the change came the loss of the 45° side vents, replaced with a bonnet-length scoop along the top of the side panel.

Under the bonnet, old or new, there have been several changes in engine capacity; 1949 - 375cc, 1954 - 425cc, which increased the car's maximum speed from 43 to 49mph. 1970 - 435cc; the engine first used in the Dyane takes its place in the 2CV4. Also 1970 - 602cc; the Ami engined version is called the 2CV6.

The interior of the 2CV has always been renowned for comfort - not in the plush or exclusive sense, but in terms of all round pleasant-to-ride-in adequacy. Early upholstery was grey, but by 1955 it was possible to buy a version sporting a blue tartan-effect material. The bench-type seats could be removed and used as chairs. There was little in the way of instrumentation: an ammeter and a speedometer which was strapped to the pillar of the windscreen. There was no ignition key until 1953, and no demisting device until four years later.

The mid-seventies suffered a craze for modernisation - off with the old and on with the new. Goodbye to the round `eyes' and hello to more functional looking rectangular headlights, more in the Dyane/Ami tradition. But not for long. Six years on, the eyes had it again - back by popular demand! The first 2CVs were rather sparse in the lighting department; only one rear and one stop lamp. Flashing indicators were not introduced until 1955.

Fortunately, the front windows, hinged half way down, flapped open easily enough for hand signalling. and the paying of tolls - not on motorways then, but on bridges and through tunnels. Visibility gradually improved with the years. Until 1957, the rear window measured approximately half the width of the back of the car, then it expanded to almost full width. 1966 brought a third side window, which also improved the level of light for rear seat passengers.

The first 2CVs had a canvas hood, which rolled right back to the rear window. The lower section rolled upwards to beneath it. This operation could only be performed from the outside, and was a fingernail-risking exercise. From 1957 the hood was made of a plastic material, and a bootlidded version became available too.

Some of these changes represent only minor modifications, while others are important visual landmarks in the 2CV's genealogy. In particular, the old style bonnet and the lack of a third window mark out a car as a veteran!

There is one group of cars that have their own set of idiosyncrasies - these are the

The old and the slightly newer; the bonnet has changed, and along with it the shape of the grille and the positioning of the chevrons.

cars built in Citroën's Slough factory entirely for the British market with British quirks of habit in mind. The first of these cars rolled off the production line in 1953. The French might be happy to stick an arm through a flapping window to indicate intent to turn, but these cars had semaphore arm indicators, sited just to the fore of the front door. They were self cancelling, no less - a feat achieved by means of a pneumatic time switch. The rear windows opened in exactly the same way as the front ones - never an option in cars built elsewhere. From the start they also came fitted with bootlids, although of a different type. They were smooth and unribbed, and sat slightly proud of the back of the car. They carried the distinctive 'Citroën' script logo from the Traction Avant, which was also manufactured at the Slough

factory. There were special hubcaps for the British taste too. However, one of the most distinctive and obvious additions is the badge which sits each side of a raised metal 'nose' on the front of the bonnet. The legend 'Citroën Front Drive' on a blue circle around a yellow disc is joined by a futuristic front wheel design. The cars were produced in Slough until 1960. It would be another four years before Citroën began to build and export right hand drive 2CVs to Britain.

Cars with older-style bonnets have distinctive side air intakes, which add to the overall corrugated appearance.

1957; the colour is grey, the doors hinge from the central pillar and there is no third side window ...

... thirty years on, anything goes colourwise; a change in legislation moved both door hinges to the front from December 1964, and the third window appeared two years later.

The round beady-eyed headlights, here on a car of 1957 vintage, helped the 2CV get its 'duck' nickname.

Rectangular lamps came later – more modern maybe, but better?

Back, by popular demand – the eyes have it!

One step at a time - despite many minor changes, the 2CV is still the same basic shape - and still holds the same affectionate place in the hearts of its admirers.

The canvas or plastic cover made load carrying easier, but bootlids were a very popular change when they were introduced in 1958.

A 2CV engine receives attention from sisters Chantelle and Heidi Jones, mechanics at Ray Williams' workshop.

The modern 2CV interior. Hardly luxury, but comfortable and well appointed.

A Slough-built car shows its unique 'nose' badge. This is one of the few Slough cars that survive - it is owned by Sussex 2CV in Brighton.

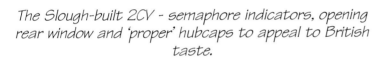

The Slough-built 2CV - semaphore indicators, opening rear window and 'proper' hubcaps to appeal to British taste.

An early car, owned by Sussex 2CV - resplendent in black.

On British-built cars the speedometer was centrally positioned; on French cars it was to be found strapped to the door pillar.

HIGH STYLE

7

In 1984, Citroën published an edition of their bilingual magazine *Double Chevron* with a portfolio of photographs by David Sparrow. Two of those pictures had been part of a portfolio that had won David the 3rd Olympiad of Colour Photography organised by the German magazine *Leica Fotografie*, confirming him as a 'Master of the Leica'

He says: "The 2CV was the first car that I ever approached as a design concept. It is a gallery of shapes on wheels. I already had quite a collection of 2CV pictures when I shot these - this was the first occasion when I had photographed models with cars. For me, cars are about people, indeed, part of the raison d'etre of the 2CV is to carry people in comfort. There are plenty of cars around which seem to have been designed without people in mind! In my choice of people, I was able to express the sense of style that 2CV ownership can be all about. It is a car with no social pretensions - one that transcends all class barriers. Returning to the 2CV ten years after this portfolio, I am more than ever convinced that it represents an inexhaustible fund of design-related images."

The 'Double Chevron' pictures, on this page, the facing page and the following four pages, are a set of six and are here reproduced together for the first time.

A smart car will reflect every facet of its owner's
personality ... and the owner those of his car.

Once upon a time, when folk should have known better, it
was commonly believed that Citroen would never stop
making the Duck. It became
fashionable to drive around
in 2CVs covered in dents.
Perfectly good wings would
suddenly have the boot put
in, in the name of fashion.
'Panel beating' became a
whole new game. Maybe as
removing dents is such an
art, creating them was
trying to be one too!

Such wanton self-indulgence should not be compared to the real battle scars of the Parisian veteran ...

... or the lop-sided charm of the Provencal workhorse.

Whether to choose a yellow car, or a black car, or perhaps a black and yellow car? ...

... or for complete contrast, red and green?

*Whatever the colour choice,
in the style stakes, the 2CV
still points the way!*

Dear Reader,
We hope you enjoyed
this Veloce Publishing
production.
If you have ideas for
other books on Citroën,
or other marques, please
write and tell us.
Meantime, Happy
Motoring!

Postscript

The photographs in this book were made over a number of years, with a number of cameras, all Leicas with the exception of a dozen which were taken with a Hasselblad.

My first Leica was a Leicaflex, and it changed the way I saw the world. I can offer no explanation for this change other than that, because it was a totally manual, selective-metering camera, it was rather slow and methodical to use, and it is quite possible that this enforced leisurely pace made me think differently. As time went by, I added a second 'flex, and later changed them both for all-electric R4s, which would take a motor-drive. I found that, although these cameras were capable of being used fully automatically, I much preferred to use them in the manual mode.

When, some years later, Leica brought out the manual-only R6, I was soon to make the change. All my original lenses fitted all the later cameras. I have added to them over the years, so that the range covers 16mm fisheye to 560mm long focus.

My favourite film is Kodachrome, which works very well indeed with Leica lenses.

David Sparrow